4/09

Our Nation's Pride

The Capitol Building

By Darlene R. Stille
Illustrated by Todd Ouren

Content Consultant:
Richard Jensen, Ph.D.
Author, Scholar, and Historian

magic Wagon

Text by Darlene R. Stille
Illustrations by Todd Ouren
Edited by Patricia Stockland
Interior layout and design by Nicole Brecke
Cover design by Nicole Brecke

Library of Congress Cataloging-in-Publication Data
Stille, Darlene R.
  The Capitol Building / Darlene Stille ; illustrated by Todd Ouren ; content consultant, Richard Jensen.
     p. cm. — (Our nation's pride)
  Includes index.
  Audience: Ages 4-10.
   ISBN 978-1-60270-112-0
 1. United States Capitol (Washington, D.C.)—Juvenile literature. 2. Washington (D.C.)—Buildings, structures, etc.—Juvenile literature. I. Ouren, Todd, ill. II. Jensen, Richard J. III. Title.
F204.C2S75 2008
975.3—dc22

                         2007034066

Table of Contents

A Very Special Building

There is a big, white building on a hill. It has a dome on top. It is the Capitol of the United States. The hill is called Capitol Hill. The Capitol is in Washington, D.C. This is the capital city of the United States. Washington, D.C., is where the nation's leaders meet.

The Capitol building is famous. People all over the world know about the Capitol and its dome. It is a symbol. It stands for the United States. It stands for laws that keep people safe and free.

5

What Is the Capitol For?

The Capitol is for people who make laws. The people who make laws are called the Congress.

Congress has two groups. One group is called the Senate. The other group is called the House of Representatives.

6

Three Parts

The Capitol has three parts. Long stairs go up to all three parts of the Capitol. The center part is round. The dome is on top of the center part. There is a statue on top of the dome. It looks like a woman. It is called the *Statue of Freedom*.

The two other parts are on each side of the round center. The parts are called wings. There is a north wing and a south wing.

9

The Rotunda

The Rotunda is a beautiful, round room. It is in the center of the Capitol. It has statues of presidents.

The walls have eight big paintings. The paintings tell stories about U.S. history.

The Rotunda has a tall ceiling. This tall ceiling is the inside part of the dome.

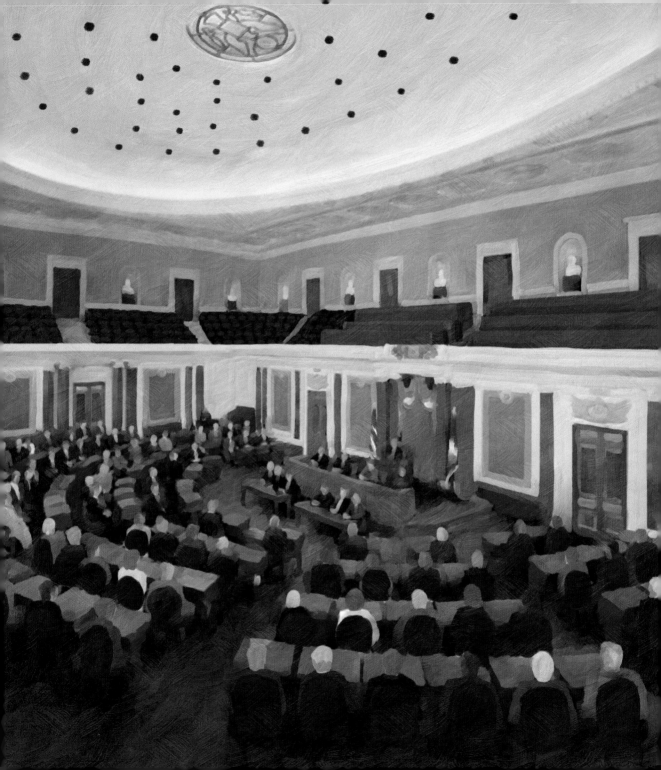

The Wings

The north wing is for the Senate. People in the Senate are called senators. Voters in each state elect two senators.

Senators meet in a room called the Senate Chamber. They also have offices in nearby buildings.

13

The south wing is for the House of Representatives. States with lots of people have more representatives than states with fewer people.

The representatives meet in a room called the House Chamber. They also have offices in nearby buildings.

How Congress Got Its Home

   In the late 1700s, when the United States was a new country, Congress met in many cities. George Washington was the first president. He wanted Congress to meet in Washington, D.C. He also wanted a building for Congress.

   Thomas Jefferson had an idea for a contest. It would find out who could make the best building plan. People sent in pictures of their ideas. A doctor named William Thornton won the contest.

Construction of the Capitol building began in 1793. Workers finished the north wing first. Congress started meeting there in 1800.

Next came the south wing. The House moved there in 1807. It would have been a noisy place to meet. Workers pounded nails and sawed boards. The south wing was not done until 1811.

War and Fire

War broke out in 1812. The war was between Great Britain and the United States. They fought in Washington, D.C. British soldiers set fire to the Capitol.

The Capitol was made of stone. Fire did not hurt the walls. The fire burned everything inside, though.

21

Two Domes

Workers fixed the Capitol. They built the Rotunda and a dome. The dome was small. It was made of wood covered with copper. People were afraid the dome might burn. All of the repairs were done by 1826.

Workers started a new dome in 1856. It took many years to build. During that time, the Civil War broke out. President Abraham Lincoln told the workers to keep building the dome. The dome and ceiling were done in 1866.

The Capitol Grows

After the Civil War, more states joined the United States.

The new states sent more people to Congress.

The Capitol needed to grow to fit the extra people.

Workers made the wings bigger. The Senate and the House

got new chambers.

25

More Buildings Added

The country kept growing. Congress needed buildings for offices. The Capitol and nearby buildings are called the Capitol Complex. There is a park outside with many trees and flowers.

A Visit to the Capitol

Millions of people visit the Capitol each year. Tickets are free. Guides show you the Rotunda and the Old Senate Chamber.

You can also see where the Senate and the House meet now. You can see Congress in action. You can get passes to the visitor's galleries from your senator or representative. You can watch history being made.

Fun Facts

• All people who get elected president go to the Capitol. They stand in front of a big crowd. They promise to obey all U.S. rules and laws. Then, they become president. Thomas Jefferson was the first president to make this promise at the Capitol.

• The president goes to the Capitol once a year. The president makes a speech to Congress. The speech is called the State of the Union address.

• The statue on the Capitol dome is made of a metal called bronze. The statue is 19 feet 6 inches (5.9 m) tall. It is as tall as three basketball players standing on each other's shoulders!

• The statue on the Capitol dome weighs about 15,000 pounds (6,800 kg). The biggest elephant weighs almost that much.

Glossary

capital—an important city in a country or a state where leaders meet.

civil war—a war between groups in the same country. The United States of America and the Confederate States of America fought a civil war from 1861 to 1865.

copper—an orange-colored metal.

galleries—balconies where people sit to watch plays, debates, or other events.

representative—a person elected to the U.S. House of Representatives.

rotunda—a large, round room usually covered by a dome.

senator—a person elected to the U.S. Senate.

statue—three-dimensional artwork made of wood, clay, metal, or other hard material.

symbol—something that stands for something else.

On the Web

To learn more about the Capitol building, visit ABDO Publishing Company on the World Wide Web at **www.abdopublishing.com**. Web sites about the Capitol building are featured on our Book Links page. These links are routinely monitored and updated to provide the most current information available.

Index